# Unlikely

# Unlikely

Colleen Crawford Cousins

modjaji books

*Unlikely*
Text © Colleen Crawford Cousins 2016

First published by Modjaji Books in December 2016
www.modjajibooks.co.za

ISBN (Print): 978-1-928215-30-1
ISBN (Digital download): 978-1-928215-46-2

Cover artwork by Colleen Crawford Cousins
Cover lettering by Jesse Breytenbach
Layout by Fire and Lion

For Kate and Eowyn

# Contents

## Unlikely

My great great great grandfather
in 1820     a pale boy on a ship
silenced by his mother's groans     seasick all of them
the Cape of Storms and then the journey up the shipwrecked coast
the savage stories of the sailors     the food
the rankness below     he saw a whale breach
too many porpoises finning
leaping through the unending sea with a terrible purpose
the strangely human eyes
(Baines has painted the arrival
a rowing boat     green breakers     beached)
East London a rough town
cobbled streets     the Quigney
the hostile faces of the porters
clicking in their gabble          smelling of wood smoke
the hard sky intolerably blue     intolerable

His father said
we are here to build this country up     unlikely
he thought

# The first time

At two, in the narrow backyard
I look up
at the blue rectangle of sky
bisected by the clothesline's flapping squares
The sky is very deep.
For the first time, I think:
I am alive!
I am here!
And I know exactly where here is,
between the back door
and the garage wall.

# My father's hands

My father's hands were small and delicate
Such a tall man and
quick on his feet, but that's another story
You noticed his hands all the time
stretched out across the keyboard
dancing ghost crabs, lightly furred

Listen to this! Over
his left shoulder, his eager face seeks out my ear
Sunday, late July
grey smoky sky,  the light's gone,
all hands on deck my mother shouts
and bangs the kitchen door

My father, though, hurries to the piano
his hands reach out and
the chords pour back into his fingers from the keys
jazz agility, jazz jokes, jazz art
perfectly disconnected from his brain
and from his heart

# Envy

Sad child sitting in a windy yard
face uplifted, howling
large and simple as dough
give up desire, it is unprofitable
your hands are empty, clenched on nothing.
Stop crying for the moon!

Poor thing
there is a moon, but it is not for you.
It is for the others
those who are eating and smiling slant eyed
they are so knowing
they turn things over and over with their little paws
everywhere they are small and quick
storing away sweetness in their cheeks like mice
winking and winking at each other
living in shadows –

how your wanting hurts my ears!

## I've been silenced

I've been silenced by
my father's shallows
my mother's Special Branch
my teacher's full stops.
my colonel's iron bars
my husband's klap and walk away
my history's long book

I've been poisoned
I've been barked away by the first dog at the door
I've allowed my thread to break again and again.

## Caliban

Be not afeard. The isle is full of noises
My mother speaks in a hurt voice
Tossing her head    complaining I do not love her
I prefer horses    their godlike smell
And the tiny men we keep under the bed
My sister and I    at night we take them out
Barry Ding Five and Tex    and ride the range with our homunculi
Later we marry badly mothered men    in agreement however
With patricide, matricide    revolution etc
When I meet the real deal    the torturers
I see how well my mother tilled my soil    prepared my ground

# What the child still wants

What the child still wants is love.
What she means: the light of early morning, bright and clear,
Thrilling to possibility, embodied, energetic,
She can run for miles barefoot and win the sprint.
Her adults groan and wallow in their muddy furrow,
Heads down
Or gone
Or snarling
But they will be abandoned for the brightness rising.

# The messengers

I dreamed I woke at Emily's. Six men stood round my bed.
The window held the lemon tree
I closed my eyes and saw the river running back towards the sea
Wake up, said number one, and come with me

The second had a wolf's mane and a wolfish nose for blood
He smelled my guilty letters out
In that soft house of women's love he could not see my face
What's this, said number two, it's terror's place

The third held up a mirror to my frightened eye
I saw the hot car speeding north
Gum trees throwing bars across the road
The silence in the cafe at the Big Hole

Their hot eyes ran like rats all over me
I dressed and I left silently
Exile from childhood all my life
Exiled shamefully

# Pitch

Jill falls in love with Jack at first sight
she falls in love with his mother Joan too
Jill needs to be close to a powerful woman
who grows her own greens
and reads the Grundrisse

Jill goes on scripting the world
a thriller full of dramatic entanglements
her story stars Jack a dreamy awkward boy
as a revolutionary hero
let the imagination take power

Jill is helplessly in love with everything
the red post office across the road
the blue noncommittal sky with its passive floating clouds
typing a pamphlet calling on
someone to do something

Jill wants to direct Jack's movie
Joan now hates Jill and takes every opportunity
Jill is ruining Jack's chances
limiting his choices forcing him into children
Joan worries out loud

Jill and Jack run off to Africa
build mud houses have babies
Jill wants the ANC to go home and run things
so she can go home too
though she's never liked home before

Less than a year after Jill and Jack split
June whom Jack has always preferred to Jill
throws up her life in Kokstad where she has lived all along
joins Jack in a rented house in Bloekom Street
a one-way in Fairview

Jack is happy with June
Joan is happy with Jack
the plot swings back to romance
Jill finds it surprisingly hard
to star in her own movie

## Photograph, Swaziland

In the river, clothed only in my beauty
a small golden child on each hand
all rising from the blessing of the waters
in my shy glance, oblique, leaves and flowers
I see at once that the river rises in my throat
and flows down my lambent skin in python loops
through the blue hills dreaming distant
all the way to unknown Mozambique

# Gift

I dreamed you sent me flowers –
roses, unseasonable, furled,
Awake, restless, the crescent moon swinging in the green sky
I count over all your gifts at last

A wooden box, carefully hinged
a mended chair
your hands on the black dog

Your arm
the touch of your arm amazed me
I turned to you with astonishment
my flesh one flesh with all the singing creatures

O ropes of sand
How did I become enchanted?
When did I lie down to sleep?

The night was still and breathless
my husband called from the lighted doorway.

Your roses have travelled ten years to me
At last they have arrived
With open hands I receive them.
How beautiful they are!

# The work of pregnancy

Look steadily at the darkness at the pupil's centre.
The iris closes like a shutter
on the tiny germ of death.
Your body was never your own.
Wilderness has entered your life
the cry of the bush baby in the night.

Moonlight pours its cold milk on your hands.
Alone, you're shuffling your deck of cards.
You choose one, turn it over: the three of hearts
lies on the table near the wedding tree.
You are not yourself. Bone, feathers, desperate flight –
accept the death you thought belonged to others.

Lie down, you must be horizontal.
Tie your hands, your feet, your long red hair
Braid them with fine thread to grass and stone.
An insect has his road upon your arm.
Gaze back into the compound eye.
There is nothing to be done.

## 1974

Kezia was born. Snow.
The roof of the duckhouse perfect, a white octagon.
A paper moon hung in my branches
I found my lion roar.

# Long live

Your breath whistled like a bird in the night
sometimes it was imperceptible, I'd put my ear to
your mouth, slightly open, the tender prominence of
your bottom lip with the seal of our love still on it

You'd open your fanned eyes and
rising from your ribbed chest, your valiant boat,
your cry pulled so hard on the wires that bound us
your cable anchored in me, I thought my heart would burst

Outside there was snow on the ground
inside, warm milk rushed down my branches
you received it eagerly, your eyes looked into mine,
our love was fierce, its only softness was your perfect skin

It was then that I formulated my demand, my awful gift:
continue to breathe, in and out
my heart's desire, the only want I want,
is that you bury me

# Home

I look into the mirror of my hand
death is written there
in a casual scribble of lines

on that Sunday long ago I sat on Daddy's knee
the stoep of the old house held the sun
like a cupped hand holds water

we drove back through dry grass
a train howled like a lonely dog across the winter sky
no moon shone

now we walk through poor streets built on winter grass
my hands are empty
I'm looking for the Sunday house

because you walk behind me
your footsteps echo mine like an assassin's
I cannot find the way

because you walk behind me
I never look into your eyes
they slant away, they hold others dear

the stone in my passway
a child running slip-slop to the corner
three birds swooping away from the curb

let your pale long fingered palm touch mine
fit finger to finger like a glove
the torn up message whole at last

lead me to the Sunday house
the train calling
the red curtain trembling in the window

## Littoral

I am in the place where dreams don't speak
the edge of the sea when the tide is out
the waves recede
the sand shines
the gulls stand in small battalions

the wind has something to say
the wind speaks in riddles

if I'd woken earlier
if I'd come here when the moon still sailed
blinking urgent signals to the night clouds
while the stars kept on winking –

and out to sea, out to sea
past the big bass of the droning waves
I know the South Pole smiles so icy
I'm here, the end, the beginning of this rolling world
trust me when the planet turns

## Moon

We all seem to know where she is
we point dumbly
up there
somewhere
waxing and waning in the empty air

Women bleed with her
the sea who breaks the backs of iron ships with a flick of his wrist
runs up the beach with the jawbone of a whale for her
on those who have lovers that love them
she is said to smile approving
as for me
I howl for her

# The rash

Spreads like water spilling on a polished floor
a flood of feeling blood
the thirteenth fairy
the tooth mouse in my empty slipper

Under the riddle of my skin
the bees in my body start moving their wings:
I will be stung to death.
I will be shut up in a golden hexagon, all eyes
My breath will be preserved in amber
The twins within me will be stillborn
They will go back to the earth as they came,
enshrouded in a pod.

Orphan child, mouthing outside the cold glass
I will remember your name.
Open your hand clenched like a fist –
it's true I've refused you seven times seven.
Now you come back like the queen bee's messenger,
promising death in a sting
Uninvited one
you leave your message scrawled, lipstick on a mirror.
I puzzle over it.

Poison spreads within me like a question.
What is the answer?
I incline my ear.
Come out
Come out

# Artemis phones her daughter

*He sai◦: foot, boot, or◦er, city, fist, roa◦s, time, knife.*
*She sai◦: water, night, willow, rope, hair, earth, belly, cave, meat,*
*        shrou◦, open, bloo◦.*
*They both kept their promises*

(From *Marrying the Hangman* by Margaret Atwood)


Did you dream of me?
Or was it always of a man?
I see you running fast
long legged on your broomstick horse
through the winter cosmos grass
My ten year old, my girl


He took you from my forest
Promises of kisses, freedom
Gave you dishes, pots, a spade
The sun was relentless, it soured the milk
The moon was a cracked mirror
swinging in the clouded sky


He'll search the whole world over for his soul
She's disguised in every woman in a room,
on the train, the dusty street
a casual blanket on the floor –
any measures, faced with Medusa.
Small change, a wedding ring

All your high arts will not heal him
though you hide your light under his bushel
and your anxious face puts on the mask of love
Grow up, get out
Take the high road or the low
The border closes soon

Leave the ghosts mouthing at your window
wrapped in their dull mystery
Open my box of darkness
Take off your mask
Make something. Imagine.

# The ancients tell us to be small and happy

Thanks for the stone house you built
steady at anchor behind me
its glass eyes open to the life within

when the small wind of afternoon ruffles our hair
the old dog lends me his back
and the tin roof speaks to the clouded sun

under your roof like a wing
the sun makes rainbows of my mirrored coat
and pours the steam from the stove like smoke across my hand

everything is standing still in its quiet place
the baskets crouch like cats on the cracked floor
our toothbrush soldiers off duty in the blue cup at the window

all day I have remembered the injunction of the ancients:
*be small and happy*

## Words to take to a desert island

I'll take tough handy words:
Axe, knife, rope, bang
And, of course, the basics –
Fern, loam, leaf, loaf
For comfort:
Cool, cavernous, cumulous, pillow
Against loneliness,
Damask, chiton, bandeau, tango
For mental stimulation, I'll pack the puzzling
Promise, soon, and pure
To use as weeks wear on I'll bring
Baleen, billow, sheetrock, ambergris
And a few small luxuries that don't weigh much
(Sidereal, fledgling, helicon, ghee)
Oh, and I'd like to pack the (possibly impractical)
Promiscuity
Always and never (those vertical cliffs of stone)
I'll leave at home.

# Bad places to be with him

On mountains
At parties
In his bachelor rent in the windy howling
On the scorpion side of Table Mountain
In lawyers' offices
With waitresses
In marital therapists' rooms
In discussion groups
On planes
In cars
In his office
In his secretary's office
On the phone
At his sister's house
At my sister's house
With or without his mother
With any other woman
On Milnerton beach
With his colleagues
With my friends
With his friends
With my colleagues
At airports
In any branch of Pick n' Pay.

A good place to be with him
(Now I remember)
In bed     tender

## The bean child questions her fate

What wicked messenger brought me here
from your ribbed rocking  boat
suspended in the blazing air?

This darkness is heavy as soil
my white foot is furiously treading
I'm frightened mama
it's a long way down I'm falling
why have I been cursed and broken
split open?

My life is furled and folded
like an insect's wing
the sun will never turn me green

# Divorce

I

Wave goodbye to the boats in the night harbour
far away now as last night's ambiguous embrace

Surely death would taste less bitter, less estranged
than this ending, which opens like a fan
to show the darker pattern of the years

My little goddess Jealousy still guards the empty hearth
of your masked and feathered face

II

When you wrote – we are two trees, my new wife and me,
growing together, but apart, all our lives –
I saw you standing absolutely still
passive
no wind in your leaves
your roots deep in regret.
Ponderous birds settle at night in your branches like a black cloud.
Deep sighs fissure your tough bark

My new lover is like water
a river runs under his skin
his juices taste of the new world, full of itself
his rough sacks dumped in the dim corner of our room enchant me
smells I don't know
are these leaves or fruits?
Their shapes remind me of nothing, they prick my curious finger

He is in the travel business
His hair is like a wing

I never liked jewelry.
You thrust your catalogue towards me, gruff as a stone lion –
gold, gold, gold.
Now I want only this flowing of like and unlike on the dark blanket
in this plain red room

You are set thick to disagree, to force something out of me –
your gridlocked road, your tight belt, your smile like biting –

Can you say, I love my mother?

Your dry tongue barks and stammers

III
The border has been officially closed.
Diplomatic contact has ceased
The envoys have returned with their exotic keepsakes, their
        native art
There is no further trade between governments.

The country people who live in the hills ignore the mephitis
        of policy
And cross the border as they have always done
Cutting reeds across the river, celebrating marriages and the
        birth of children
Carrying small goods back and forth
They are indifferent to national ambition and historic fault

Sometimes a muffled message is exchanged between principalities
Easily decoded by the experts, it always reads:
The situation is steadily improving
The farmer is ploughing with his strong oxen
The crafter is making her life with her hands
Those that predicted disaster are proved wrong

## Saying goodbye to the ancestors

My dead, have I not piled long years on your altars,
breastfed and saved from drowning
two husbands, fresh and green?
I've balanced one block on another tirelessly
built houses which fall down, again and again

Have I not planted trees root to crown
horny barked, thorny barked,
in every country and season?
I have played you by heart, fingered your keys
When have I closed my curtain against your moon
that blanks out the night with its big zero?

Still you arrive daily on the bus
with your white faces pressed against the glass
your wooden hands stretched out, stiff as promises
how you scratch the inside of my eye
with your dry fingers, dust around your knees

Dust mounts your tyres
Do you see that I am turning away?

# The rule of two

Two births, two abortions
One white hand, one red
The door opens and closes without justice.
I should be thankful
The yes...yes to life
where do we keep them, those mysterious double islands?
My body is still too sad
I kiss my shoulder
console my arms for the death of second hope –
all those red exotic flowers, dried blood
my heart pounding till it broke.

Two sons have gone away
goodbye mother
my cupboards still full of food
lentils leaning this way and that in their glass jar, overlooked
meat rotting
tomatoes dripping in a wooden bowl.
Of course I'm bitter
Bitter as ripe lemons, the sour goodness
of any test of faith.

## Summer rain

Summer rain falls in Cape Town
mother of return, garden of remembrance
In Harare, my borrowed love, my used-to-be
a riot last week on Second Street
Kabila's war comes home
Women in ragged coats hurry through Mbare dust
Tall trees still pin slow clouds helpless to the sky
I breathed your thin air once and longed for rain

Africa for the Africans!
For me only this despairing citizenship
that comes, at last, to question with
the white eye, the vetplant, the sad baboon
my right to be here
O my country, my family of origin
my small girl, little horse, shy fish
the common octopus in her lonely pool
her eggs laid, hatched at last –
the past stops suddenly

# Crossroad

I knit my life, plain and purl. Grief and despair.
The new house, the new life starts here.

Everyone I know is on the edge of something
vertigo or bargaining
some have already jumped
their immunity compromised.
Those still married to always and never can be recognised
by the areas of deadness around their hands and feet

I gave the hungry child cous cous
and the chicken soup my mother left behind.
Her anxious eyes still light up Nothing Street.
The spider's lost and spins in jagged loops

My dead father the perfect gentleman
taught us to please and thank and spare the ants their life.
My quiet sister answered him by burning down the house.
Later she showed me how she floated
just off the ground for years after the fire

# Bushveld

Someone rises up surprised
Someone knows the answer to this wet leaf
The rain touches my face with her soft hand
The door of my skin opens
Clouds multicoloured as goats move briskly over the hill

The rain walks away on long legs
Red soil on the wall of the clinic in Phokeng
In the kloof full of darkness and water
Someone is not pleased
The buildings hurt with their tight corners

Oil makes rainbows on the roadside
The wild chainsaw of frogs working their flood
Mad excitement
The kingdom of god
here
at the tough white roots of grass

Someone's bird flies back
urgently to the other world
Will I drown in this rainy sky
Someone's eyes
Someone's door is open

## Sunflower

I say, the problem of form
you say, clouds drift across the empty sky
dying and being born

storm cloud is far from home
in my wildest whirlwind
your face turns always to the sun

each action has consequences
the butterfly moves her wing in the walled garden in Ireland
        in May
in June, a great storm off the Cape

the delicacy of your weather system!
I approach you step by step
fall at last into your circle

Sacred space, my home
your golden blessing
black hearted one

## The clouds of Georgia o'Keefe

Downtown skyline
forest of soaring towers
dwarfed by the wide skies of America!
Endless dark blue prairie
buffalo clouds drifting side by side,
woolly, pacific

This is the country of Seven Arrows!
Chicago your autochthonous call
vibrates in the throats
of the people gathered together from the four directions

As above, so below.
The people of this city
took Georgia's airplane clouds
and hung them
so that those who live
down amongst the dark roots of that soaring canopy
see how these great skies stretch from sea to sea

## Patriotism (Freedom day, 27 April)

To turn and love: my lucent ribs, my ribs that cup my eager
        fountains
my red bird beating in her frondy branches
my softness, the softness of my belly
the tender hill that rises from my braves, my hipbones
my bones that have carried me along the flood waters
for sixty years, my legs, my ankles, my dik dik
two slender birds, bright eyed, watchful
My lions. I follow their great marks in my sand.

My two hands climb and float, arboreal, clever, playful
They pleach, grasp, stir, fold and unfold, look, they know how
        to live
at the end of my arms, my faithfuls, each in her place lifting sleekly
her broad band of muscle, scarped from the shoulder, fearless,
        obedience is joy.
They are delighted, they dance, they move like lovers
clasped in one another's thoughts.

My bones turn and flutter in their jointed boxes, knees, elbows
speaking in high calcate voices, love me. Look
how we turn with the world, this way and that, wearing our
        pearly stitches like flags
we are your nation.

# Climate change

This is the burning heart of our narrow summer
Too hot to touch the steering wheel
Out of the cupboards come the bare backs
The bright flowers
The naked feet
Out of the stone wall come the scorpions
We bend over the rock pools with the children
Who are covered from neck to ankle in lycra
Because of the melanomas
Because of the bluebottles
Because the sharks have right of way on the beaches
Surely it's hotter than last year?
Reject the ecopathology of daily life.
It will be over very soon darling.

# Land reform

The train to Alicedale
Those clouds
Two blues, a complex grey
Drowse in the crooked mirror of the dam.
Her case is packed for Joburg. A child
Sleeps against the window

Biko – your  grave in Ginsburg
Our prayers float up like smoke
Women bitter as salt sit
against the warmest wall
Barefoot in her cloak
Noxolo praises you

Twenty four yokes in an empty house
The oxen are all gone
This earth is furrowed with the dead
I touched your stone cold stone

Rock art site, Salem
I can't touch you mother through this rock
You've died away into the slant of a cheekbone
Your eyes more alien than spaceships
Your hands cup change from cigarettes

Alone on this hill in Salem
My eye catches your creature
Duiker I call in answer to his name
Up here the stars are arrows
behind the winter sun

In your body mother
You flew and swam and spoke with animals
As I do in dreams
Against barbed wire and stagnant water
Tired grasses lean

Salem means broken promises
Twenty six houses mother
Their black mouths gaping saying

Rain taxi school fees pension
Nietverwacht and allesveloren
On the faint radio I pick up through the static
Agrarian tenurial restitution

# A visit to Sutherland, June 16

*1.*

gritted teeth of straight dirt roads
falter at the edge of town
then stop abruptly
as if the urban impulse had suddenly died in a distant catastrophe
and fetched up here
to desiccate in the desert air

after that there's nothing but
light pouring down from the huge blue
sharp as a butcher knife
small black shadows hide like lambs
under each of the six million grey bushes

grey bushes that stand like sheep, but lonelier
undulating in slow motion to the far horizon
waving goodbye surreptitiously
it's overwhelming   the pointillist simplicity
a kind of sea sickness

*2.*

see it sideways, mirrored in the corner of an eye
reflected off the sinkdakke,
the Algemene with its leather shoes and threadbare potatoes
(everything but milk and greens)
the cop shop (busy)
the library (empty)
only one coloured child having his life saved by literature

↘

Sutherland is seismically the calmest place on earth
the bucket system is still in place, 6 billion years later
kanol: the old word for rooted

local knowledge is puzzling
dead garden, dead volcano, dead sheep
this is the birthplace of van Wyk Louw, of Adriaan Vlok
born here but left asap
Bushmen still here, we saw
two boys playing pool at one of the three tables at Andre's
Imagine a town so poor there are no squatters

3.
15 km away is another town but we never saw it
(we were told) Japanese stargazers stay up all night
looking back in time aiming 50 mirrors
at the millions of exceptionally bright and piercing stars they
          have up there

the stars stare right back down
at the general public for a price
but it was booked up till December

# New

*I. Tiger*

Kate burns bright against my thigh
Her white hand's fearful symmetry
Against the great branch of my arm
Keeps my forest creatures warm.

*II. The catch*

Your mother and I
lie lapped in your coracle
the ebb and flow of patient milk
pulls and tugs our kitchen talk

Life takes tiny breaths.
Beneath your drifting baby frown
your wide gaze wanders to the line
between the winter sea and sky

Before our dazzled, half averted eyes
your life's bright fish run quickly in.

# Please stay

I have begun to see
The machines invented to stop time
The snapshot, going off like a shotgun
Arresting that sudden smile, your fluttering hands
Please stay
Let this moment last
But it slips out under the door, flattening itself like a snake
Leaving behind its special agents, the domestic spies
The frightening egg timer
And the clicking watch, the little death machine

## What I say on a bad day

What I say
on a bad day
is might as well, might as well stay
for the last act, perhaps the play turns to a strange conclusion,
for example the gun mentioned in the first act
sleekly threatening the audience with its familiar
much documented violence
stays on its hook in sullen silence.

# Family wedding

The wedding day was interminable
We drove and drove
Far into the Agterkaap under a hot blank sky
Luckily a good-looking man called Craig
Bought me a double gin from the Cash Bar
The guesthouse dog, unaccustomed perhaps to crowds
Or merely bored
Bit the bride's mother savagely on the thigh

The marriage officer wore a purple dress
The exact colour of the ubiquitous bougainvillea
She gave a tender talk on commitment
How we all wept!
Later I was told this talk had been written
By the 27 year old advertising executive from Chatsworth
With the coral necklace round his golden neck

Eventually the Cairo Shwarma van arrived
Toiling hotly over the billowing roads
We queued for hours, chatting amongst ourselves
As the full moon slowly rose

No not much in the way of speeches
And I withdrew before the quarrels began
Though by morning all was amicable
Except for the guesthouse owner
Who complained about making breakfast for forty people
We left him there, sulking over the scrambled eggs
And drove back at speed to the lovely city

## 2012

The plan is
To move to Angola in May and breed horses
And to finish at last the book Practical Faces (for babies)
And to take the cello again between my legs
I will reread Lessing's Canopus in Argos, all five novels
Remembering the bus ride through Cairo
When I told Thomas the whole of Shikasta, sotto voce,
While the nasal tour guide used a mic to address the five passengers
Before we went to the Ford Foundation cocktail party
In Tahrir Square.

# Found poem: Mowbray News, 15 July 2014

This is to report
that an intruder entered our property [in Alma Road] this
    afternoon.
I saw a figure peering in at a side door, and found this woman in
    the drive –
I cannot understand how she got in.

She was very strange

had a long tale about having been discharged from hospital
insisted on raising her clothes to show dreadful open wounds
and sank to the ground moaning.

My guest and I persuaded her to leave
having unfortunately given her some money.
Our domestic worker said she had seen this woman often in
    Pillans Road.
It seems that she may have been the same woman who came a
    few days ago, and swore at our neighbour.
She was going down the road ringing all the bells.

Is she part of a gang?

By chance, Mr Jannie van der Mescht [of ADT] was passing,
    and he asked one of his security officers to call round.
We reported the case.
The woman did not manage to get into the house
but we do not know how long she had been wandering around
    outside.

# Found internet poem: Ruby is broken

Ruby is fundamentally broken.
Ruby can be made to do the job with enough effort and pain
But Ruby is still broken.

I occasionally find a useful post that
leads me around a crater-like pothole.
But the standard documentation is sparse to
the point of uselessness, and often misleading.

The standard library is a pile of crap.
There is a timeout class that will helpfully
allow you to wrap whatever you want in a timeout
that uses Ruby's (broken) threads in an (even more) unsafe way.
It throws an exception that is outside the usual hierarchy
and must be explicitly caught or it takes your app down.

Instead of raising an exception,
the time-string parsing function
will return to the current time if it can't parse a string.
How do you tell if you've managed to correctly parse a string?

The community is hostile and unhelpful.
I have tried twice to submit patches. The first was ignored.
I was interrogated about the other until
I convinced the other guy that it was a problem
at which point I was ignored.

The language is badly designed.
Library imports have been Done Right (to varying degrees)
in a large number of completely dissimilar languages.
Ruby uses something similar to C
which makes tracking down where anything comes from
        a nightmare.
The ability to reopen classes makes it impossible to know
if you're ever looking at the whole of something.
In general, you're probably not.

The heavy dependence on magic
is a little short-term convenience at the cost of massive,
        long-term pain.
Use of Ruby's inflexible meta-programming features is strongly
        encouraged.
This results in code that is hard to debug, almost impossible
        to understand
and has all sorts of weird interactions with everything.

# Cadmium

Cadmium is my weakness
I am strongly attracted
but as my brush dives
slight frown –
didn't I have trouble with you before?
Troublesome cadmium

Cadmium comes up from the mine in buckets
men in tin hats
candles, yellow fumes
deep dangerous
cadmium too much on my brush,
on my mind

Families are so challenging
Cadmium's daughter green
another difficult customer
Cadmium and green in each other's arms
lighting up the dark corner
I shake my head

Cadmium and blue meet on the sly
happiness too perfect
made for each other
their blowsy green takes after both of them
plump smiling blue and
wicked cadmium

Celestial blue, cerulean sky
I'd like to dive into, drown in you
nothing so wonderful
your planet spinning, hit badly once
knocked, rocks about
(part of its charm), winter spring etc

Sudden yet regular flushes & blushes
snow creeps down, flung back
tidal wave of white blossom
rushes towards the equator
falls off suddenly
early October, then the fruit

Starts as a dark dot in the eye
concentric layers, cadmium, your apricots
your mangos, your bananas
but lemon yellow lemon
that touch of bitterness, your estrangement
you're so hard to get along with

# On turning sixty

Notice how her coat lies abandoned.
The arms have shrugged and given up
It seems they have lost their ambition.
Her shoes lean towards each other, commiserating in tiny voices.

I would like to draw your attention
to the dust on top of the fridge
also to the dust on the light bulbs, and the dust in the recesses
of the wooden doors.

There is evidence that leaves have shuffled through the gap
under the front door
Avoid trampling them
they squeak like dying mice.

Follow the beckoning drip drip
to the bathroom. Please note the tap's persistence
has achieved a calcium ring
This bath is slowly turning back to stone.

Now raise your eyes to the window
observe the brightness undiminished
applaud the wild embrace of pear and bouganvillea
on the roof of the stoep, which softly bends
and leans to their embrace.

Plants have cracked their pots and stepped into the world
The grass has realised its ambition.

## Nobody asks anymore

How is the old man?
Is he still breathing, opening
eyes soft as an elephant's
on this quiet room?
Do the children still come to sit with him
touch his clawed hands
two tortoises asleep on the blue duvet
Graca and Zelda, two stone lions at the door?

# Mvuleni

On this mountain
the first water to fall as rain
followed with natural intelligence
every subtle angle of decline
the easiest way down
in its longing for the sea

All rain since
has favoured this wise path
the path of no resistance
without effort it cuts mother rock with its soft knife
into creases, deep kloofs
rain gently breaks the mountain into tiny pieces

The rain becomes a river
shouldering aside rocks in its rush
for its somnolent lagoon
its stony crocodiles and busy prawns
its estuary breathing in and out in perfect timing with the sea
it releases at last its red memory of mountain soil
opening like a fan into the bay

Printed in the United States
By Bookmasters